TAKE TEN YEARS

1940s

Published by Evans Brothers Limited
2A Portman Mansions
Chiltern Street
London W1M 1LE

© Ken Hills 1991

First published 1991
Reprinted twice
© in this edition 1996

Typeset by Fleetlines Typesetters, Southend-on-Sea
Printed in Spain by GRAFO, S.A. - Bilbao

ISBN 0 237 51681 0

Acknowledgements

Maps – Jillian Luff of Bitmap Graphics
Design – Neil Sayer
Editor – Caroline Sheldrick

For permission to reproduce copyright material the author and
publishers gratefully acknowledge the following:

Cover photographs – Popperfoto; Topham

page 4 – (from top) Popperfoto, The Hulton Picture Company, The
Vintage Magazine Co, The Vintage Magazine Co; page 5 – (from
top) The Vintage Magazine Co, Topham, Popperfoto, The Hulton
Picture Company, Barnaby's Picture Library; page 9 – (top) The
Hulton Picture Company, (bottom) Ronald Sheridan/Ancient Art &
Architecture Collection; page 10 – The Fine Art Society, London/
Bridgeman Art Library; page 11 The Vintage Magazine Co; page 12
– The Vintage Magazine Co; page 13 – (top) The Vintage Magazine
Co, (bottom) Topham; page 14 – (top) The Hulton Picture
Company, (bottom) Topham; page 15 – The Vintage Magazine Co;
page 16 – Topham; page 17 – e.t.archive; page 18 – Topham; page
19 – (top) Topham, (bottom) The Hulton Picture Company; page 20
– (top) The Vintage Magazine Co, (bottom) Popperfoto; page 21 –
(top) The Vintage Magazine Co, (bottom) Imperial War Museum,
London/Bridgeman Art Library; page 22 – (left) Topham, (right)
The Hulton Picture Company; page 23 – The Hulton Picture
Company; page 24 – The Vintage Magazine Co; page 25 – (top)
Topham, (bottom) The Hulton Picture Company; page 26 – The
Hulton Picture Company; page 27 – (top) The Vintage Magazine
Co, (bottom) Topham; page 28 – Topham; page 29 – The Vintage
Magazine Co; page 30 – (left) Barnaby's Picture Library, (right)
Topham; page 31 – Barnaby's Picture Library; page 32 – Topham;
page 33 – Topham; page 34 – (top) Topham, (bottom) The Hulton
Picture Company; page 35 – Topham; page 36 – Topham; page 37 –
All-Sport Photographic Ltd; page 38 – (top) Richard Gardner/
Barnaby's Picture Library, (bottom) The Vintage Magazine Co;
page 39 – Topham; page 40 – Topham; page 41 – Topham; page 42
– Topham; page 43 – (top) The Hulton Picture Company, (middle)
Topham, (bottom) The Hulton Picture Co; page 44 – The
Advertising Archives; page 45 – The Advertising Archives

The author and publishers would like to thank Trans World
Airlines, Inc. for permission to reproduce the advertisement at the
top of page 44.

TAKE TEN YEARS
1940s

KEN HILLS

EVANS BROTHERS LIMITED

Contents

Introduction – Theme chart for the forties   6 – 7

1940 The 'phoney war' ends with the invasion of Norway and Denmark. Churchill forms a British National Government, Germany invades Holland, Luxemburg and Belgium, and France. German troops force Allies onto the beaches at Dunkirk, where they are rescued. The Battle of Britain is fought in the skies.   8 – 11

1941 Germany invades Russia, but troops are halted by fierce winter weather. The Japanese attack Pearl Harbor. Rommel advances in the north African desert.   12 – 14

1942 The Germans reach Stalingrad, but are trapped there. Japanese forces make huge gains in south-east Asia. The Allies defeat Rommel at El Alamein. The RAF bombs Cologne.   15 – 17

1943 Germany is defeated at Kursk in Russia. German forces surrender in north Africa. The Allies invade Italy but are halted at the Gustav Line. America attacks strategic islands around Japan.   18 – 20

1944 The Allies have Eisenhower as their new commander. The Normandy landings begin a new phase of the war. Paris is liberated. The Allied advance is halted by a surprise attack at Ardennes. Soviet troops advance to Warsaw, but the German garrison stamps out the Polish uprising there. The Red Army takes several Balkan countries for Russia.   21 – 23

1945 Allied soldiers reach Berlin. Hitler commits suicide. Mussolini is executed. Germany surrenders. Liberating troops see the horrors of the Nazi concentration camps. London celebrates VE Day. Japan fights on until Hiroshima and Nagasaki are destroyed by atom bombs. Japan surrenders.   24 – 27

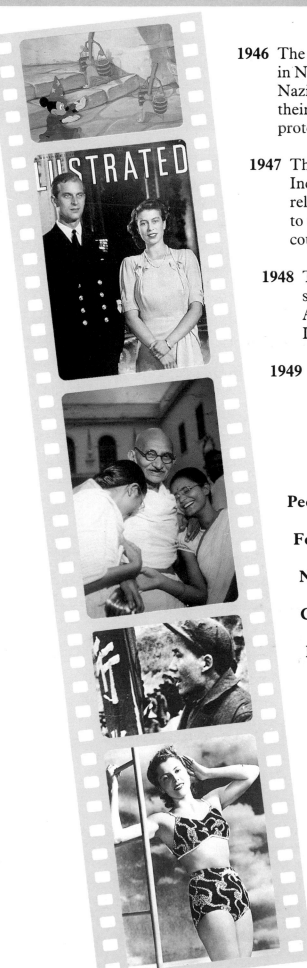

1946 The United Nations is founded, and given a home in New York. War trials in Nuremberg condemn Nazi criminals; ten are hanged. The French assert their control in Vietnam; it is resisted. Zionist Jews protest in Palestine.   **28 – 30**

1947 The last viceroy is sent to India to prepare for Independence. British rule ends in India, amid a religious bloodbath. America promises financial aid to war-ravaged Europe, though not to Communist countries.   **31 – 34**

1948 The state of Israel is born. Israelis fight for survival. Russia blockades Berlin and the former Allies airlift in supplies. Gandhi is assassinated in India. Britain has a new National Health Service.   **35 – 38**

1949 Palestinian Arabs flee from new Israeli territory. Russia lifts the Berlin blockade. Mao Tse-tung and his Communists march into Peking, and declare the People's Republic of China. South Africa elects the Nationalists on an Apartheid ticket. NATO is formed.   **39 – 41**

People of the forties   **42 – 43**

For the first time ever   **44 – 45**

New words and expressions   **45**

Glossary   **46**

Further reading   **46**

Index   **47**

The pictures on page 4 show
Winston Churchill
American bomber-pilot
Russian mud stops the Nazis
Aboard the *Missouri* as Japanese delegates assemble to surrender

The pictures on page 5 show
Mickey Mouse as The Sorcerer's Apprentice in *Fantasia*
Princess Elizabeth and Lieutenant Philip Mountbatten
Gandhi and his granddaughters
Mao Tse-tung
The new bikini

Introduction

The forties were dominated by World War II. It was the most costly and destructive war in history and its effects, for good and ill, were felt far beyond the battlefields. Over 55 million people died; about 15 million combatants, the rest civilians. Many of these died from bombing; more died in concentration camps, or from hunger and disease.

After the war was over, millions of people were left homeless. In western Germany alone, one in five of the population was a 'displaced person'. Some had fled from the east of Germany when the Russian army arrived; others were slave workers from countries Germany had conquered, brought to Germany to work in mines and factories. From all parts of Europe, Jews who had survived the holocaust flocked to Palestine in the hope of founding a Jewish state there.

In Britain, the old class system had been steadily decaying since World War I. The working classes had seen that their rulers were not their 'betters', and challenged their right to rule. More people had a chance of education; there seemed hope that life would improve. Despite wartime hardships, in countries like Britain which were not actually invaded, many people's lives changed for the better. Men who would never normally travel abroad saw sights which changed their outlook. Rural life took on more importance as farms tried to feed the whole population. Women stepped easily into men's shoes and won new respect. Throughout Europe, people's view of the world changed because of the war.

The same was true in those African and Asian countries under the control of various European empires. In the first years of the war the colonial powers suffered crushing defeats. They were humiliated in the eyes of their colonial subjects. After the war, there was no going back. One after another, the colonies won their independence. The story of these new countries was beginning to unfold at the end of the decade. The European powers had lost their empires and owed vast sums of money to America, which emerged as the most powerful nation, along with the Soviet Union. The entire world seemed to line up on either side with one of these 'superpowers', under the dread shadow of the atomic bomb.

YEARS	WORLD WAR II
1940	The phoney war German blitzkrieg overwhelms Allies Dunkirk miracle: British army saved Battle of Britain
1941	German army invades USSR Winter halts German advance Japanese attack Pearl Harbor See-saw in the desert
1942	Battle of Stalingrad Japanese capture Singapore Alamein: Britain's desert victory RAF mounts first 1000 bomber raid
1943	Kursk, the gigantic battle Allies beat Axis in desert war Hard fighting in Italy Japan: the ring begins to close
1944	D-Day: the invasion of Europe Allies reach the Rhine The Red Army's year of victories Japanese disasters in the Pacific
1945	Battles rage in Berlin Germany surrenders Atom bomb destroys Hiroshima Japan surrenders. End of the war

YEARS	WORLD AFFAIRS
1946	New York home for UN UN bans the atom bomb An 'iron curtain' divides Europe War danger in Vietnam
1947	US saves Europe with Marshall plan Millions die as India becomes free Truman pledges aid against Reds
1948	East and West squabble over Germany Russians blockade West Berlin Anglo-American airlift saves Berlin Burma wins independence
1949	Russians lift Berlin blockade NATO alliance to protect the West UK crisis: pound sterling devalued Apartheid established in South Africa

OTHER NEWS	WARTIME ALLIANCES		
Churchill becomes prime minister Stalin crushes all opposition US voters pick Roosevelt again Chaplin mocks the Dictators	**1939** **Sept 1** Germany invades Poland **Sept 2** Britain and France issue an ultimatum to Germany threatening to declare war unless Germany withdraws Germany does not reply Within a week, the following countries declare war on Germany: Britain and Britain's colonies Australia New Zealand South Africa Canada France and all French colonies		
Air heroine Amy Johnson missing Women called up Night blitz on British cities Walt Disney's fantastic *Fantasia*	**Sept 17** Russians invade Poland		
French suffer under German occupation Church bells ring for Alamein Utility clothing launched in Britain	**1940** **April 9** Germany invades Denmark and Norway; by **June 9** both have surrendered **May 10** Germany invades Belgium, the Netherlands and Luxemburg. By the end of May all three sign a truce with Germany		
Slaughter in Warsaw's ghetto Allied leaders plan road to victory Social security scheme in Mexico	**June 10** Italy declares war on Britain and France **June 22** France and Germany sign an armistice **Sept 27** Germany, Italy and Japan sign pact		
Hitler survives bomb plot United Nations planning meeting	**1941** **June 22** Germany invades Soviet Russia **Dec 7** Japan attacks Pearl Harbor **Dec 8** USA, Britain and the British Commonwealth and Empire declare war on Japan **1943** **Sept 3** Italy surrenders to the Allies		
Roosevelt's death shocks Allies Labour wins British election Allies rule a divided Germany China torn by civil war	**1945** **May 7** Germany surrenders to the USA and Britain **May 8** Germany surrenders to Russia **Aug 8** Russia declares war on Japan **Aug 15** Japan surrenders to the Allies		

WARS	PEOPLE	EVENTS
Palestine: Jews attack British British Palestine HQ blown up China torn by civil war	Nazi leaders executed Goering escapes the gallows TV pioneer John Logie Baird dies Juan Peron elected in Argentina	No end to British food rationing More US atom tests in the Pacific The 'bikini' explodes in Paris
British rule in Palestine to end UN to take over in Palestine UN votes to divide Palestine	Mountbatten: India's new viceroy London's royal wedding Car-maker Henry Ford dies Heyerdahl's epic voyage	Britain and America freeze up 'New look' in women's fashions Giant computer starts up Food rations cut in Britain
Last UK troops leave Palestine Jews declare state of Israel War as Arabs invade Israel	Gandhi, India's peacemaker, killed Truman re-elected US president Princess Elizabeth has a son	Olympics begin again – in London Free medicine for all Britons
Israel and Arabs sign armistice China: Communists win civil war	Mao Tse-tung, China's new master Orwell's nightmare novel *Nineteen Eighty-Four*	British pound devalued by a third Clothes rationing ends in Britain Better sound – if you can afford it

1940

March 3	Stalemate in war with no fighting
May 10	Churchill forms National Government
May 13	Germans advance into France
June 4	Miraculous rescue of allied troops from Dunkirk
June 19	Fall of France
Aug 20	Battle of Britain

THE WAR IN EUROPE
STALEMATE

March 3, London   Britain and France declared war on Germany six months ago, when Germany invaded Poland. Their armies face each other ready for war, but so far there has been no fighting. In Britain they call it a Phoney War. The German name for it is 'Sitzkrieg', the Sit-Down War.

WAR BUILD-UP

May 10, Oslo, Norway   German forces invaded Norway and Denmark in April. The Danes were taken completely by surprise and surrendered. There was fierce fighting around Oslo, the Norwegian capital. A Norwegian Nazi named Quisling announced that he now rules the country on behalf of the German invaders. Now, most of Norway is controlled by the Germans. British and French troops landed by the Royal Navy have failed to drive them out. Both the Germans and the British have lost ships in battles at sea along the Norwegian coast.

CHURCHILL REPLACES CHAMBERLAIN

May 10, London   Neville Chamberlain has been forced to resign as prime minister of Britain. He has been criticized for feeble leadership and blamed for Britain's failure to save Norway from the Germans. Winston Churchill replaces him, and is forming an all-party National Government.

GERMANS OVERWHELM ALLIED ARMIES

May 13, France   Hundreds of German tanks are advancing into France. They have burst through the French defences and are moving rapidly west and north. This advance follows three days after Germany's invasion of Holland, Luxemburg and Belgium. The German airforce (the Luftwaffe) controls the skies over the battlefields. The French and British are making hurried plans to fight back.

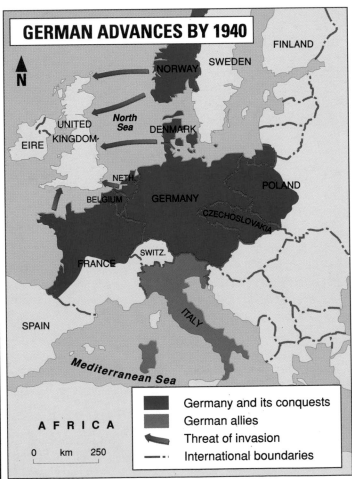

GERMAN ADVANCES BY 1940

Germany and its conquests
German allies
Threat of invasion
International boundaries

By 1940 the Germans had taken much of Europe.

BRITISH SURROUNDED IN DUNKIRK

May 29, France German tanks have reached the Channel coast and cut the Allied forces in two. The British army is trapped in the port of Dunkirk. The only way out is by sea. Hundreds of little ships are streaming across the Channel from Britain to rescue the troops lined up on the shore.

MAGIC DOWN A RABBIT HOLE

Nov 1, Lascaux, France Some French boys out catching rabbits have stumbled across one of the most remarkable discoveries of our time. They came across a gap in some rocks, hidden by undergrowth. They climbed in and found themselves in a cave. The cave walls and ceiling were covered in brilliant pictures of prehistoric animals and their hunters. Experts say the pictures are 15,000 years old.

A MIRACULOUS RESCUE

June 4, London The ships that went to Dunkirk have brought back to Britain over 300,000 men. Many of the troops have been saved but all their weapons and equipment have been lost. For the time being, the British are without an army.

Allied soldiers queue for transport at Dunkirk.

A bull and horses in Lascaux caves, France.

BRAVE DE GAULLE FIGHTS ON FOR FRANCE

June 19, London France has been crushed. Paris is in German hands and the French Government has fled to Bordeaux. Further military resistance in France is pointless. But some of the French are determined to fight on from abroad. Their leader is a junior member of the French Government, General Charles de Gaulle. 49-year-old de Gaulle flew to London yesterday. He was taken to see Prime Minister Churchill, and later made a broadcast appeal to the French people. "The flame of French resistance must not, and shall not die," he told them.

THE RAF UNBEATEN

Aug 20, London The Luftwaffe and the RAF are fighting a fierce war in the air over southern England. German troops are waiting to invade Britain, and their airforce must destroy the British defences first. Both sides have had many aircraft shot down but the RAF is unbeaten and full of fight.

HITLER CALLS OFF THE INVASION

Sept 19, London In air battles on September 15 the RAF claims to have shot down 185 German aircraft. The Luftwaffe has failed to overcome the RAF. Hitler has given up his invasion plans. The RAF has saved Britain. Churchill has said "Never in the field of human conflict has so much been owed by so many to so few".

The Battle of Britain, by Paul Nash

NEWS IN BRIEF . . .

STALIN'S REVENGE

Aug 21, Mexico Leon Trotsky, one of the revolutionaries who brought Communism to Russia, is dead. Yesterday a young Spaniard, who had pretended to be a friend, plunged an ice-pick into his head.

Trotsky was expelled from Russia in 1927 for daring to oppose the Russian leader, Stalin. He finally settled in Mexico, but never ceased to criticize Stalin in his books and his speeches. Now Stalin has silenced him, for there is no doubt that the killer was acting on Stalin's orders.

WHAT BRITONS ARE SINGING

Jan 31, London Many famous songs came out in the last, Great War. The most popular songs at the moment are 'Roll out the Barrel', 'We're going to Hang out the Washing on the Siegfried Line' and 'Run, Rabbit, Run'.

TRAGEDY IN THE ATLANTIC

Sept 22, London The ship *City of Benares* was full of children. It was sailing to America to take them away from the dangers of war in Britain. Reports have now come in that a German submarine has sunk the *City of Benares*. Ships have picked up 46 children; 306 are believed to have been lost.

THE CHILDREN COME HOME

Jan 30, London When war broke out last September, thousands of city children were sent to live in the country where they would be safe from bomb raids.

Parents missed their children and many children did not like living in the country. Gradually they have returned to the cities. Three in four have now gone home.

ROOSEVELT WINS AGAIN

Nov 5, Washington, USA American voters have chosen Franklin D. Roosevelt to be their president, for the third time. Roosevelt is the first American president to serve a third term in office.

PETS AT WAR

"Send your pets to the country if you can. If you cannot, remember that your dog will not be allowed to go into a public air raid shelter with you. So don't take him shopping with you. Take him for walks near home, so that you can get back quickly.

When you take him into your own shelter with you, put him on a lead. If you can get a muzzle for him, you should do so, because he may get hysterical during raids. Put some cotton wool in his ears. Ask your chemist to mix a dose of bromide all ready for you to give him when a raid starts.

Cats can take care of themselves far better than you can. Your cat will probably meet you when you get into the shelter."

(BBC broadcast on care of pets in wartime Britain.)

SHOCKING CONDITIONS UNDERGROUND

Sept 30, London Thousands of Londoners are spending their nights at their local Underground station to shelter from the bombing. It is the safest place to be. An East End girl says:

"When you get over the shock of seeing so many sprawling people, you are overcome with the smell of humanity and dirt. Dirt abounds everywhere. The floors are never swept and are filthy. People are sleeping on piles of rubbish. The passages are loaded with dirt. There is no escaping it.

There they sit in darkness, head of one against feet of the next. There is no room to move, hardly any room to stretch . . ."

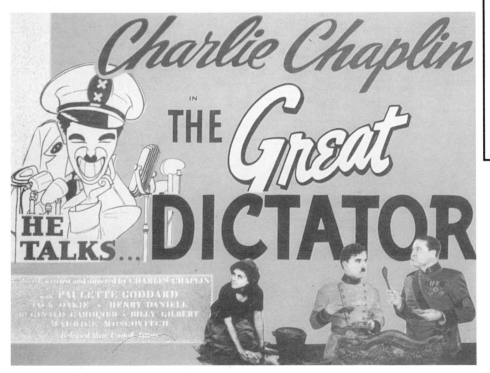

THE GREAT DICTATOR

Nov 11, London Charlie Chaplin's new film *The Great Dictator* is showing in London. In the film, Chaplin pokes fun at Germany's dictator Adolf Hitler. He plays the part of a comic dictator, Adenoid Hynkel, dressed up in Nazi-style uniform, and made to look very like Hitler.

1941

April 11   Benghazi falls to Afrika Corps
May 27   The *Bismarck* finally sunk
Dec 2   Invaders freeze in Russian winter
Dec 7   Japanese bomb Pearl Harbor

RUSSIA INVADED

Oct 26, Moscow   In June, Hitler launched a gigantic attack on the Soviet Union. Three million men, with 7000 guns and 3000 tanks, poured into Russia on a front 2000 km (1240 miles) long. They soon overran the city of Minsk, 320 km (198 miles) inside Russia. Soviet commanders were bewildered by the speed of the German advance, and Stalin ordered that anything which might be useful to the enemy must be destroyed. Under this 'scorched earth' policy, crops are burnt, livestock killed and all machinery destroyed. But the Germans heading for the Soviet capital, Moscow, are facing a new enemy – mud. Rain and heavy traffic have churned the dirt roads into knee-deep mire. Anything on wheels becomes bogged down. Worse is to come: the days are growing colder and the first snows of winter have fallen.

INVADERS FREEZE IN RUSSIAN WINTER

Dec 2, Moscow   Thousands of German soldiers are frost-bitten and their equipment is frozen solid. Hitler's armies are at a standstill. Fresh Soviet troops from Siberia, equipped to fight in cold weather, have joined in the battle for Moscow. They have begun a huge attack on a front 960 km (377 miles) long. The Germans are retreating.

THE WAR AT SEA

May 27, North Atlantic   Battered by the guns of the Royal Navy, the *Bismarck* finally went down at 10.39 a.m. today. The huge German battleship threatened to create havoc among the convoys bringing essential supplies to wartime Britain. About 100 survivors have been picked up. At least 2000 men have gone down with their ship.

The End of the Bismarck, by Charles E. Turner.

US FLEET CRIPPLED

Dec 7, Honolulu, Hawaii Japanese aircraft have bombed the US fleet in a surprise attack on the naval base of Pearl Harbor. They have caused immense destruction and over 2000 soldiers, sailors and civilians have been killed. The fleet will be out of action for several months. Britain has joined the United States in declaring war on Japan.

Japanese bombers create havoc at Pearl Harbor.

JAPAN'S BLITZKRIEG

Dec 25, Hong Kong Japan has made spectacular progress since attacking Pearl Harbor. Japanese forces have landed in Thailand, Malaya and the Philippines. They have seized the US island of Guam and today, after a brave defence, Hong Kong has fallen to them.

WAR IN THE DESERT

April 11, Libya Earlier this year, British and Commonwealth forces advanced 800 km (500 miles) against the Italian army facing them in the North African desert. Germany's Afrika Corps has now replaced the Italians. Commanded by General Erwin Rommel, the Afrika Corps has launched a violent attack. Benghazi has fallen, and 20,000 Allied troops are cut off in Tobruk.

ANZAC TROOPS STRANDED

May 24, Wellington New Zealand's Prime Minister Peter Frazer is worried about the morale of his country's fighting men. The Australians feel the same, and have complained to Churchill about the lack of air cover when these 'Anzac' troops are advancing. After the lost Battle of Crete, many of the troops left stranded on the island were Australians and New Zealanders. Many were taken prisoner of war. Some have gone into the hills, where they are sheltered by local Cretans.

AFRIKA CORPS RETREATS

Dec 10, Libya The Commonwealth 8th Army is advancing against the Afrika Corps. Tobruk has been freed and Rommel has been pushed back to where he started out last April.

WOMEN CALLED UP

Dec 30, London An appeal for women war workers went out in Britain in March. Now, even more help is needed in factories and the Government has conscripted all women aged 20 to 30. Some will join the services, others will do vital war work.

Land girls are replacing many male farm workers who have joined the forces.

NEWS IN BRIEF . . .

AMY JOHNSON MISSING

Jan 8, London Amy Johnson is feared drowned. She was flying a new aircraft to deliver it to an RAF airfield when its engine cut out. The plane came down in the mouth of the Thames and there has been no sign of Miss Johnson since. Amy Johnson made history on a solo flight from Britain to Australia before the war.

THE FIRST BOY SCOUT DIES

Jan 8, London Lord Baden Powell has died aged 83. He became a hero for defending the town of Mafeking in 1899 and 1900 in the Boer War, in South Africa. He will be remembered for founding the Boy Scouts in 1908 and the Girl Guides in 1910.

COMFORT UNDER LONDON'S STREETS

Feb 28, London At dusk, as the last travellers depart, London's Underground stations fill up with families who have come to shelter from the bombing. There is less queuing for places now. Conditions are much improved. People can sleep three deep on the platforms since the Government put in bunk beds. Several stations have been equipped with cookers and kettles to provide hot food and drink. Regular shelterers have organized knitting or sewing parties and there are story-telling groups for the children. When morning comes the Underground returns to normal. The police clear the shelterers out of the stations ready for the first passengers to arrive.

BRITAIN AND AMERICA SIGN AN ATLANTIC CHARTER

Aug 14, London At a secret meeting at sea, President Roosevelt and Prime Minister Churchill have agreed their aims in war and peace. The war will go on until their enemies have been defeated. Once peace comes, all people must be able to live free from fear and want under a government of their own choice.

The agreement is to be called the Atlantic Charter.

Roosevelt and Churchill met aboard HMS *Prince of Wales*.

THE BLITZ

May 31, London Nearly four million of the 13 million houses in British cities have been damaged by German bombing. 200,000 have been completely destroyed. Many thousands of people are homeless. They are living in any temporary shelter they can find.

FANTASTIC FANTASIA

Nov 30, Hollywood, USA Walt Disney has made an entirely new kind of film. *Fantasia* is a concert of famous pieces of music, each one illustrated by a cartoon. In one, Mickey Mouse plays The Sorcerer's Apprentice.

1942

May 10	Surrender of US in Philippines
May 31	A thousand bombers raid Cologne
Aug 31	German tanks advance to Stalingrad
Nov 2	British victory at El Alamein
Nov 23	Germans trapped at Stalingrad

STALINGRAD THREATENED

Aug 31, Stalingrad, USSR German tanks have entered the outskirts of Stalingrad. Most of the city is in ruins and 40,000 of its people have been killed in air attacks by the Luftwaffe. The German High Command is confident that Stalingrad will fall easily in a few days.

GERMANS TRAPPED

Nov 23, Stalingrad After months of desperate street fighting, Stalingrad is unconquered. It is encircled by the Russian Red Army. The 250,000 German troops still fighting there are under constant attack and are dying of cold and hunger. They cannot hold out much longer.

Wrecked houses in Stalingrad.

Ruins in the heart of the city.

An abandoned gun awaits capture.

German troops advance through destroyed buildings.

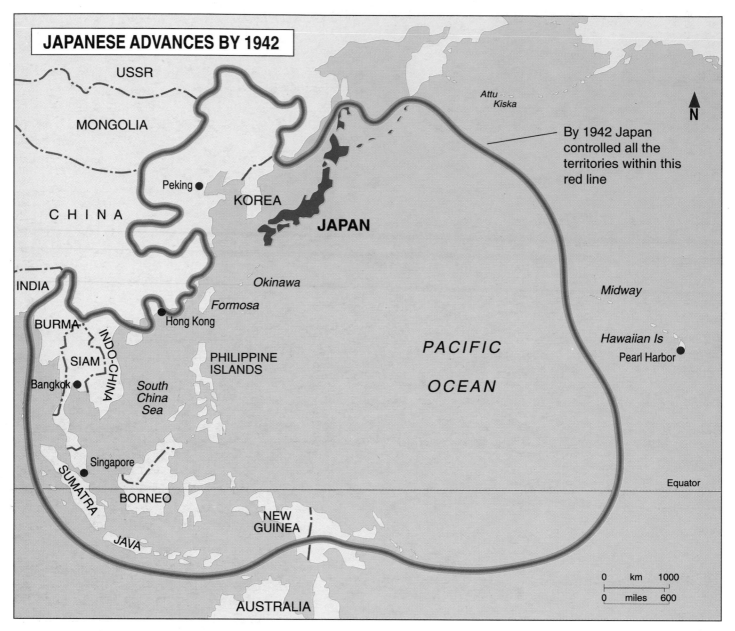

JAPANESE ADVANCES BY 1942

By 1942 Japan controlled all the territories within this red line

JAPAN MARCHES ON

May 10, Philippines Japanese armies have scored success after success in the Pacific and south-east Asia. The Japanese force which landed in Malaya captured Singapore in February. The Japanese have also overrun the Dutch East Indies; they have occupied Burma and threaten India. Today the last US troops have finally surrendered the Philippines.

BRITISH VICTORY AT EL ALAMEIN

Nov 2, Cairo, Egypt After a 10-day battle the Afrika Corps under Rommel has abandoned El Alamein. This is where the Germans halted after a 350 km (137 mile) desert trek. The British 8th Army, under its new commander General Montgomery, is pursuing them westwards.

General Montgomery confers with his colleagues.

A THOUSAND BOMBERS RAID

May 31, Cologne More than a thousand RAF bombers attacked the German city of Cologne last night. They caused widespread destruction. This is the first thousand-bomber raid of the war and easily surpasses in weight and ferocity anything the Germans threw against British cities last year. It is unlikely to be the last.

THE LONG ROAD BACK

Dec 31, Pacific Ocean The Americans have begun the long slow task of driving the Japanese from the conquests they have made since Pearl Harbor. In June, US ships and aircraft destroyed a Japanese fleet in a battle off Midway Island. Now, US marines are fighting desperately to recapture Guadalcanal, one of the Solomon Islands.

NEWS IN BRIEF . . .

MAKE DO AND MEND

May 1, London Clothing has been rationed in Britain since last June. Every item of clothing has to be bought with coupons. A year's ration is 66 coupons, and is enough to provide everyone with their basic needs. Fashion in clothes, such as people enjoy in peacetime, is impossible. Everybody has to make do and mend.

GERMANS LOOT FRANCE

June 30, Paris The French people watch helplessly as the German conquerors continue to take everything they want from France. A black market flourishes but at prices only the well-off can afford. Food and clothing are strictly rationed. Disease among children is growing because of their poor diet. Few cars are running because petrol is almost unobtainable. Coal and wood needed for heating are in very short supply and all but the rich dread the coming winter. The French are a beaten nation and they are not allowed to forget it. A strictly enforced curfew begins every evening at 8 p.m. and goes on until 6 a.m. the next morning.

JAEGER

The best in Utility

DRESSING TO ORDER

June 30, London The war has hit the fashion industry. Trouser turn-ups, pocket flaps and fussy pleats will all disappear under the Government's Utility scheme. Any fashion detail seen as unnecessary will be done away with. They use up too much cloth in times of shortage.

Some of the top names in the fashion business have been taken on to design Utility garments. Hardy Amies, Hartnell and Molyneux are among the famous designers who will dress the nation at reasonable prices. Britons may have to cut their clothes to suit the war effort, but they will still be smart.

There are also plans to introduce Utility furniture.

SAVE FUEL IN WARTIME

February, London Fuel is short in wartime Britain, so people are urged to use less hot water. They are asked to take fewer baths and to keep the level of the water down to five inches (13 cm).

MOTORING STANDSTILL

June, London In Britain, no new motor cars are being made while the war is on. There is no petrol at all for private motoring. Many people are travelling by bicycle instead. In America, petrol has been rationed to three gallons a week.

MALTA WINS GEORGE CROSS

April 16, Malta The Mediterranean island of Malta has been awarded the George Cross after suffering continued bombardment by German aircraft.

VICTORY PEALS

Nov 15, London Church bells are ringing in Britain today to mark the victory at El Alamein. They have not been heard since the invasion scare of 1940. The Government at the time ordered that church bells should be rung only for one reason – as a warning that the Germans had landed. They have been silent ever since.

1943

May 13	Surrender of Germans in north Africa
July 25	Germans lose the Battle of Kursk
Sept 3	Allied troops invade Italy
Dec 31	Gustav line halts allied progress in Italy

THE TIDE TURNS
THE BATTLE OF KURSK

July 25, Russian Front   The German invaders have suffered their greatest defeat in the Russian campaign. The German High Command planned to slice off a great bulge in the Soviet line at Kursk and trap everything inside it. A million German troops with tanks and aircraft were hurled into the battle but could not pierce vast Russian defences. There was a triple ring of anti-tank positions, minefields and fortifications around Kursk. For the first time in the war a blitzkrieg-style attack has failed. It is a turning point in the war.

GERMAN ARMY IN RETREAT

Dec 31, Russian Front   Last month the Red Army retook Kiev, the ancient capital of the Ukraine. In the past year, the triumphant Russians have advanced more than 300 km (186 miles) and are halfway to driving the enemy out of their country. The Germans are in retreat.

INVASION OF ITALY

Sept 3, Messina   Units of the 8th Army have landed in southern Italy. For the first time since Dunkirk, the Allies are fighting on the mainland of Europe. They are faced by a German army. The Italian Government is seeking an armistice with the Allies to take Italy out of the war.

The British 8th Army's Bailey bridge over the Sangro River in Italy.

VICTORY IN NORTH AFRICA

May 13, Tunisia The German forces in Africa have surrendered. General Arnim, who replaced Rommel in March, gave up the fight in north Africa today. Last month, leading troops of the two Allied armies linked up in Tunisia. The Afrika Corps was trapped between the Allies and the sea.

THE WAR AGAINST JAPAN

Dec 29, Solomon Islands Japanese soldiers do not surrender; they fight until they are killed. One after another, the islands that ring Japan are falling to the US forces, but every metre of ground has to be fought for and American losses are very heavy.

GUSTAV LINE HALTS ALLIES

Dec 31, central Italy The Americans and British have made slow progress up the Italian peninsula in the teeth of determined German resistance. They are now held up by the Gustav Line, a chain of German defences across Italy.

BIG THREE IN PERSIA

Nov 28, Tehran The three Allied leaders, Stalin of Russia, Churchill of Britain and Roosevelt of the United States, are meeting in Tehran in Persia to plan the next moves in the war against Germany.

Stalin, Roosevelt and Churchill in Tehran.

NEWS IN BRIEF . . .

FINAL GHETTO ASSAULT

June 30, Warsaw, Poland On April 19, German troops entered that part of Warsaw called the ghetto, in which Jews have been imprisoned. The Jews, already wretched with hunger and illness, fought for a month until they were totally exhausted. Seven thousand Jews died in the fighting. The 56,000 who survived have been herded into specially-built concentration camps.

Polish Jews from the Warsaw ghetto are rounded up by German troops.

"ALL FOR ARMS AND ARMS FOR ALL."

RAGS

BONES

PAPER

OLD TIME TABLE 1934

THE THREE SALVAGEERS.

A poster showing salvage workers as the Three Musketeers.

A UNIQUE REGIMENT

June, London The 93rd Searchlight Regiment is staffed entirely by women. Their main job is to light up enemy aircraft so that British night fighter pilots can see them and shoot them down. Another task is to use their lights to show the way to badly-damaged bombers returning from raids over Europe. One after another, the beams from the searchlight batteries beckon the crippled aircraft toward airfields where it is safe for them to land.

Women operating seachlights of the Anti-Aircraft Command.

SAVE PAPER – SAVE CARGO SPACE

June 30, London No newspaper in Britain is to be more than four pages long. The Government has issued this order to save paper.

MEXICANS RECEIVE STATE HELP

September, Mexico City Mexico is one of the poorest countries in the world, but has just adopted a system of social security. If a Mexican earns wages regularly, he can use the system. There is free medical and surgical care, hospital treatment, old-age and death benefits, and free adult education. A poster in the new social security building advises: 'Take care of yourself; Mexico needs you.'

1944

Jan 16	Eisenhower appointed supreme commander
June 6	Allies invade Europe at Normandy
Aug 26	Liberation of Paris
Oct 9	German garrison massacre Warsaw Poles
Oct 26	Huge Japanese losses in Leyte Gulf
Dec 12	Appalling losses in Pacific war
Dec 16	Germans counter-attack in Ardennes

INVASION OF EUROPE
SUPREME ALLIED COMMANDER APPOINTED

Jan 16, London US army general Dwight D. Eisenhower, known as 'Ike' to his soldiers, led the joint American and British invasion of north Africa. He will head the huge Allied force assembling in Britain for the invasion of Europe.

THE GREAT ASSAULT

June 6, 'D-Day', Normandy Early this morning, the first Allied troops waded ashore on the coast of France in the face of fierce German resistance. By this evening they had set up several secure bases along the shore. Allied ships and aircraft have been hammering the German troops and defences.

GERMANS LOSE 60,000 MEN

Aug 20, Falaise, France On August 2, American armoured forces broke away from the Normandy beaches. They advanced rapidly and threatened to cut off the Germans still locked in battle with the British at Caen. 10,000 died in the battle and 50,000 are trapped around the town of Falaise.

The Landing in Normandy, Arromanches, D-Day Plus 20, June 26 1944, by Barnett Freedman.

SOVIET ADVANCE NEARS WARSAW

July 31, near Warsaw, Poland   The once-unbeatable German soldiers are in constant retreat. They were overwhelmed by the speed and power of the Russian assault when the Red Army began its summer offensive. The Germans have been driven from Russia and now hold a line along the River Vistula, close to Warsaw, the capital of Poland.

PARIS HAILS DE GAULLE

Aug 26, Paris   Paris is free. As was right and proper, Free French soldiers were the first Allied troops to enter the city. But today belongs to the man who has kept French resistance alive throughout the war, General Charles de Gaulle. Today, General de Gaulle led Free French and American troops on foot through 24 km (15 miles) of cheering crowds to the heart of Paris. He and his officers, together with a vast throng, then joined in a thanksgiving service in Notre Dame cathedral.

THE ITALIAN CAMPAIGN

Dec 9, Rimini   British and American forces have pushed back the Germans to a front winding across northern Italy and are now digging in for the winter. The war in Italy has become a sideshow. Allied forces here are being disbanded and many units are being transferred to the main battlefront on the borders of Germany.

SLAUGHTER IN WARSAW

Oct 9, Warsaw   It is believed that 200,000 Poles, most of them civilians, have been killed in Warsaw. When the Red Army reached the River Vistula, the Poles in Warsaw rose against the German garrison. They acted too soon. The Germans beat off Soviet attempts to break through to the city. In revenge, they massacred the Polish population and destroyed every building left standing in the city.

The ruins of Warsaw after the uprising.

SHOCK ATTACK STUNS ALLIES

Dec 16, German border   A massive German counter-attack has rocked the Allied armies poised to cross the River Rhine. Early this morning, a huge artillery barrage descended on the American positions in the Ardennes forest. Tanks and infantry following up have overrun the dazed defenders.

GERMAN ADVANCE HALTED

Dec 26, Bastogne, Belgium   American paratroops have fought off every attempt by the German counter-attack to seize this key town. The German advance is faltering as Allied forces prepare to recapture the ground they have lost.

THE GREATEST SEA BATTLE

Oct 26, Leyte Gulf, Philippines In a battle lasting three days, the American Pacific fleet has damaged the Japanese navy so severely that it is unlikely to take a major part in the rest of the war. The Japanese losses are four carriers, three battleships, 19 smaller vessels and 10,000 men.

Earlier this year, Avenger torpedo aircraft and the new Hellcat naval fighter won a great victory in the Philippine Sea. In a two-day battle, the Americans destroyed 600 Japanese aircraft and sank two aircraft carriers.

THE RED ARMY'S YEAR OF VICTORIES

Dec 1, Belgrade, Yugoslavia As the Red Army advances, it is founding a new Soviet empire in Eastern Europe. As they drive the Germans out of the Balkans, the Russians are replacing governments friendly to Germany with puppet rulers controlled by the Soviet Government in Moscow. Romania, Bulgaria and Hungary have fallen under Soviet influence. A month ago, Soviet troops liberated Belgrade, the Yugoslav capital, where another pro-Russian government has been formed.

APPALLING COST OF PACIFIC WAR

Dec 12, Philippines The US airforce is now able to bomb the Japanese mainland from bases in the Mariana Islands captured earlier this year. These successes and others elsewhere in the Pacific have been won with great loss of life. The main strength of the Japanese navy was used to crush the US navy at Leyte. The Japanese used 'kamikaze' or suicide tactics: pilots, dedicating their lives to the Emperor, crashed their aircraft on US warships.

Japanese kamikaze pilots before their last flight.

NEWS IN BRIEF . . .

ARRIVAL OF THE PREFABS

April 30, London To help relieve the housing shortage, prefabricated houses are being made. The first of the 500,000 to be built were shown in an exhibition today.

The steel-framed units each have two bedrooms, a living room, bathroom, WC and compact kitchen. Everything is cleverly designed to save space.

The prefabricated houses, known as prefabs, will be used to house bombed-out families and soldiers returning from war.

NEW PEACE-KEEPING BODY

Sept 16, Quebec The Allies are planning for a better world when the war is over. President Roosevelt and Mr. Churchill have agreed to start work on an organization for keeping the world at peace. It will be called the United Nations Organization.

HITLER ASSASSINATION FAILS

July 21, Berlin An attempt by a group of German officers to kill Hitler has failed. The bomb planted in his headquarters went off, but Hitler was saved by the thick wood of a table. Several of the plotters have been shot. Others are being held for trial.

BAND LEADER FEARED DEAD

Dec 16, New York Glenn Miller, the famous band leader, is feared dead. His plane disappeared on a flight to France where he was due to appear. Glenn Miller and his orchestra have played in war zones in the Pacific, the UK and Europe, cheering the troops with favourites like 'In the Mood'.

DADS ARMY STANDS DOWN

Nov 11, London Today the Home Guard was disbanded. The 1084 battalions were formed in 1940 when Hitler looked set to invade England. Many Home Guard members have been active in anti-aircraft duties.

1945

March 26   Japan bravely defends Iwo Jima
May 1   Hitler commits suicide
May 8   Germany surrenders; VE Day
June 22   Americans win Okinawa
Aug 7   Hiroshima destroyed by A-bomb
Aug 15   Japan surrenders

WAR ENDS IN EUROPE
ALLIES ACROSS THE RHINE

March 31, River Rhine   Both the Americans and the British and Canadians have made crossings of the Rhine. They are preparing for an attack on Germany which will link up with the Russians and end the war in Europe.

BATTLES RAGE IN BERLIN

April 24, Berlin   The Red Army was the first of the Allies to reach the German capital, Berlin. The city is completely surrounded but the Red Army is being made to fight for the city street by street. Hitler and his closest followers are gathered in a vast underground shelter in the city. Hitler still believes that Germany can win the war, and gives orders to armies that no longer exist. He has about a million men to defend Berlin. Many are under-age and half trained, some are old men, and all are short of ammunition. The Russians and their British and American allies have complete command of the war. The German airforce, so vital to the war, has ceased to exist.

TWO TYRANTS DIE

May 1, Berlin   Hitler is dead. He committed suicide yesterday in his underground bunker in the heart of Berlin. Three days ago, his great ally Mussolini was captured and shot by Italian partisans.

A SUICIDAL DEFENCE

March 26, Iwo Jima   This small rocky island, within easy flying distance of Japan, has finally fallen to American marines. Iwo Jima was defended by 22,000 Japanese soldiers. Of these, 216 survived to be taken prisoner. The rest died in the fighting.

Raising the Russian flag over the Reichstag, the government building, in Berlin

GERMANY SURRENDERS

May 8, Rheims, France   Yesterday, officers of the German High Command surrendered to the Allies at General Eisenhower's headquarters in Rheims. Today, they signed surrender terms with the Soviet Command at Karlshorst. The war in Europe is over. The war with Japan continues.

Allied soldiers liberating concentration camps were horrified by what they saw. This boy was at Belsen.

LONDON CELEBRATES VICTORY

May 8, London   Today is Victory in Europe Day: VE Day for short. The Prime Minister spoke to the nation on the wireless at 3 p.m. and the King is to broadcast at 9 p.m. tonight. The centre of London is packed with people singing, dancing, shaking hands and hugging each other. The royal family has spent most of the afternoon on the palace balcony waving to the cheering thousands below. In Whitehall, the centre of Britain's Government, an enormous throng called for Prime Minister Churchill. When he appeared they sang 'For He's a Jolly Good Fellow'. Flags are out everywhere and the crowds are streaming towards Piccadilly, in central London, for a night of celebration.

Britain went wild on VE Day.

BELSEN CONCENTRATION CAMP LIBERATED

April 15, Belsen   "Next day some men of the (Oxfordshire) Yeomanry arrived. The people crowded around them kissing their hands and feet – and dying from weakness. Corpses in every state of decay were lying around, piled up on top of each other in heaps. There were corpses in the compound in flocks. People were falling dead all around, people who were walking skeletons . . . .

About 35,000 corpses were reckoned, more actually than the living. Of the living, there were about 30,000 . . . .

The camp was so full because people had been brought here from east and west. Some people were brought from Nordhausen, a five-day journey, without food. Many had marched for two or three days. There was no food at all in the camp, a few piles of roots (vegetables) – amidst the piles of dead bodies. Some of the dead bodies were of people so hungry that though the roots were guarded by SS-men they had tried to storm them and had been shot down. There was no water. . .

I went into the typhus ward, packed thick with people lying in dirty rags of blankets on the floor, groaning and moaning. By the door sat an English Tommy talking to the people and cheering them up. They couldn't understand what he said, and he was continually ladling milk out of a cauldron. I collected together some women who could speak English and German and began to make records. An amazing thing is the number who managed to keep themselves clean and neat. All of them said that in a day or two more, they would have gone under from hunger and weakness.

The next morning I left this hell-hole, this camp. As I left, I had myself deloused and my recording truck as well. To you at home, this is one camp. There are many more. This is what you are fighting. None of this is propaganda. This is the plain and simple truth."

(Derek Sington, political officer, reported by Patrick Gordon-Walker in *Book of Reportage*, Faber 1987)

A FORGOTTEN WAR

May 19, Thailand border The British and Indian troops of the Fourteenth Army have driven the Japanese from their foothold in India, cleared them out of Burma and now stand poised to invade Thailand. This ferocious campaign in the jungle, led by the British General 'Bill' Slim, has been one of the most brilliantly-fought of the war. It has been little noticed. The struggles in Europe and the Pacific have dominated the headlines.

SLAUGHTER AT OKINAWA

June 22, Okinawa Okinawa is the base the Americans need for the invasion of Japan. It has taken them three months of the bloodiest fighting to capture it. American commanders estimate that if the Japanese defend Japan as they have fought for Okinawa, the final attack will cost a million American casualties.

HIROSHIMA DESTROYED

Aug 7, Washington, USA A new, and most terrible kind of bomb has been dropped on the Japanese city of Hiroshima. It exploded into a gigantic, purple ball of fire. A huge, dark cloud, shaped like a mushroom, rose from it. The single atomic bomb was dropped by an American B29 Superfortress yesterday. Most of the city and thousands of its inhabitants have been wiped out by this new and devastating weapon. In a nation-wide broadcast, America's President Truman has spoken of the atomic bomb. He threatened the Japanese with "a rain of death" unless they agreed to surrender.

JAPAN SURRENDERS

Aug 15, Tokyo On Aug 9, a second nuclear bomb struck Japan. A large area of the target, the port of Nagasaki, was laid waste and thousands of its citizens died amid the ruins. The Emperor of Japan has told Japanese armed forces and people that Japan had no choice but to surrender to avoid complete destruction. World War II is finally over.

HIROSHIMA DESTRUCTION OBSERVED

Sept 9, Hiroshima "Suddenly a glaring whitish pinkish light appeared in the sky accompanied by an unnatural tremor which was followed almost immediately by a wave of suffocating heat and a wind which swept away everything in its path.

Within a few seconds the thousands of people in the streets and the gardens in the centre of the town were scorched by a wave of searing heat. Many were killed instantly, others lay writhing on the ground screaming in agony from the intolerable pain of their burns. Everything standing upright in the way of the blast, walls, houses, factories and other buildings, was annihilated and the debris spun round in a whirlwind and was carried up into the air. Trams were picked up and tossed aside as though they had neither weight nor solidity. Trains were flung off the rails as though they were toys. Horses, dogs and cattle suffered the same fate as human beings. Every living thing was petrified in an attitude of indescribable suffering. Even the vegetation did not escape. Trees went up in flames, the rice plants lost their greenness, the grass burned on the ground like dry straw."

(Marcel Junod, *Warrior without Weapons*, Jonathan Cape 1951)

NEWS IN BRIEF . . .

SUDDEN DEATH OF PRESIDENT

April 12, Washington, USA President Roosevelt died suddenly today. He was having his portrait painted when he complained of a blinding headache. Two hours later he was dead. Vice-President Harry S. Truman automatically takes Roosevelt's place. He has rarely been in the public eye, but those who work with him say that only Roosevelt knew more about the war than he does.

LIGHTING-UP TIME AGAIN

July 15, London The blackout in Britain is over. Streets, shops and public buildings are lit up as they were before the war. Some children, who are seeing these bright lights for the first time, are said to be terrified by them.

RESTRICTIONS LIFTED

July 31, London During the war there were many things the British were not allowed to do. Most of these bans have now been lifted. Today Britons may use a car radio, buy a large-scale map, sound a factory hooter and release a racing pigeon without police permission.

CIVIL WAR IN CHINA

Oct 11, China Talks between Mao Tse-tung and the Nationalist leader Chiang Kai-shek to unite China have collapsed and China is in the grip of civil war. It is ten years since Mao's Communist Red Army escaped from the Nationalists into northern China.

NATIONS UNITE FOR PEACE

Oct 24, New York The United Nations Organization has been formally established. Twenty-nine nations have signed the United Nations Charter, hoping to prevent war in the future.

LABOUR LANDSLIDE!

July 26, London The Labour Party, led by Clement Attlee, has won the British election by a big majority. The Tories under Churchill have been defeated.

The logo of the new United Nations.

GERMANY AND BERLIN TO BE DIVIDED BETWEEN ALLIES

Aug 2, Potsdam, Germany Germany is to be controlled by troops of the countries that won the war. A meeting at Potsdam to decide the areas to be occupied has just ended. Russia will take over the eastern half of Germany.

The rest of the country will be run by the Americans, the British and the French. The German capital, Berlin, lies in the Russian sector. It has been divided into four zones, each to be controlled by one of the powers.

1946

Jan 10	Inaugural session of United Nations
July 22	Zionist outrage in Palestine
Oct 16	Ten Nazi war criminals executed
Nov 23	French bomb Vietnam
Dec 14	United Nations bans use of A-bomb

EAST-WEST TENSION GROWS
THE UNITED NATIONS

Jan 10, London On this day 26 years ago, the League of Nations was founded. Today its successor, the United Nations Organization, is holding its opening meeting. The Belgian Foreign Minister, M. Paul Henri Spaak, has been elected President of the General Assembly, but only by a single vote. He was supported by the United States and her allies in the West. Soviet Russia and the Communist states of the East failed to get their candidates elected.

This difference of opinion is all part of the ill will and suspicion that has grown up between the wartime allies.

OUTRAGE IN PALESTINE

July 22, Jerusalem Part of the King David Hotel, the British government and military headquarters in Palestine, has been blown up by a time bomb; 42 people are known to be dead.

The Jews want the British out of Palestine in order that they may set up an independent Jewish state. The attack is believed to be the work of Jewish Zionist terrorists.

NAZI WAR CRIMINALS CONDEMNED

Sep 30, Nuremberg, Germany The wartime allies set up a tribunal to try the Nazi leaders for war crimes. It has now announced its verdicts. Eleven war criminals, including Hermann Goering, have been sentenced to death; eight have received long prison sentences; two have been acquitted.

Prisioners await the verdict at Nuremberg.

WAR BREWING IN VIETNAM

Nov 23, Vietnam French aircraft have bombed the port of Haiphong in the north of Vietnam, a former French colony. In March, France gave Vietnam independence, but as part of the French Union of nations. A resistance movement, the Viet Minh, has sworn to get rid of the French altogether. They are supported and armed by China. The Viet Minh control large areas in the north of the country. The French attacked Haiphong in an attempt to destroy the Viet Minh's main link with the outside world.

IRON CURTAIN FALLS

March 5, Fulton, USA "A shadow has fallen upon the scenes so lately lighted by the Allied victory . . . From Stettin on the Baltic to Trieste on the Adriatic, an iron curtain has descended across Europe."

(Sir Winston Churchill)

EUROPE IN 1946:THE COMMUNIST BLOC

N

FINLAND

NORWAY SWEDEN

North
Sea

DENMARK

EIRE

UNITED
KINGDOM

USSR

NETH.

GERMANY POLAND

BELGIUM

CZECHOSLOVAKIA

FRANCE SWITZ. AUSTRIA

HUNGARY

ROMANIA

YUGOSLAVIA

SPAIN ITALY

BULGARIA

Mediterranean Sea

0 km 250

—— The 'Iron Curtain'
☐ Communist Bloc in 1946

GOERING ESCAPES THE GALLOWS

Oct 16, Nuremberg Ten Nazi war criminals died on the gallows this morning. Missing was Martin Bormann, Hitler's deputy who disappeared in the last days of the war and has never been found. Hermann Goering also cheated the hangman. He committed suicide by biting a cyanide pill hours before his execution was due.

THE UN BANS THE BOMB

Dec 14, New York All 51 members of the United Nations have voted to ban the use of the atomic bomb and other weapons of mass destruction.

The United Nations want to prevent another destructive atomic explosion.

NEWS IN BRIEF . . .

THE 'BIKINI' EXPLODES IN PARIS

September, Paris A bathing costume has caused a sensation at the autumn fashion shows in Paris. The outfit is very small indeed, and has been nicknamed a 'bikini' after the island site of the atomic explosion test in the Pacific earlier this year. According to the designer, the bikini and the bomb have a similar explosive effect.

The new bikini has taken Paris by storm.

DEATH OF TELEVISION PIONEER

June 14, Bexhill-on-Sea, England The death has been announced of Mr. John Logie Baird, the television pioneer. He was 58. In 1926, Mr. Baird became the first person to show pictures by television of moving objects.

FOOD RATIONING CONTINUES

Feb 7, London The House of Commons has been given the gloomy news that food rationing in Britain is to get worse rather than better. The rations of butter, margarine and cooking fat are to be cut, and there is no hope of more meat or eggs. A world food shortage is to blame, the Commons were told. Yesterday, the Ministry of Food issued a recipe for squirrel pie!

ARGENTINA HAS NEW LEADER

Feb, Buenos Aires The rule of the army in Argentina is over. A free election here has made Juan Peron president. Peron has been a popular Minister of Labour in the military government.

Peron promises to give power back to the working people of Argentina. He will increase their wages, and nationalize banks and railways. He has also promised Argentinian women the vote.

HINDUS AND MOSLEMS RIOT IN INDIA OVER INDEPENDENCE PLANS

Aug 19, Calcutta Thousands of Indians have been killed in days of fighting between Moslems and Hindus. The Hindus support the British plan for a new government of all India. The Moslems demand their own independent state.

The rioting was ended when British troops opened fire on the mobs. The situation is now said to be 'under control'.

Lord Wavell (left, pointing), Viceroy of India, inspects riot damage in Calcutta.

1947

Feb 28   The New Look launched in Paris
June 5   Marshall Plan to aid allies
Aug 15   Independence for India and Pakistan
Nov 20   Princess Elizabeth marries

INDIA'S NEW VICEROY

Feb 20, London   Lord Louis Mountbatten is to be the new viceroy of India. He will also be the last, for the British Government has made it clear that Lord Mountbatten's task is to steer India toward national independence. Power is to be handed over to the Indian people not later than June 1948. The country will remain a parliamentary democracy.

Lord Mountbatten was wartime commander of Allied forces in south-east Asia, and is related to Britain's royal family.

THE BIG FREEZE

Feb 20, London   Britain is in a chaotic state after weeks of freezing temperatures and days of blizzards. The shortage of coal for power stations has reduced the electricity supply. Thousands of factories are without power and four million workers are idle or on short time. Trains and their passengers have been stranded in the snow, and many main roads are blocked for miles by huge snowdrifts. It has been a hard winter in America too. In December, New York was hit by blizzards which left the city under a metre of snow.

IT'S A COLD WAR

April 17, New York   Mr. Bernard Baruch, former adviser to President Roosevelt, has given us a useful phrase to describe the state of world politics today. In a speech yesterday in South Carolina, he said that relations between the Western powers and the Soviet bloc amounted to a 'Cold War'.

NEW LOOK IN WOMEN'S FASHIONS

Feb 28, Paris   Designer Christian Dior has caused a revolution in women's clothes with his spring collection. Women love his shapely dresses with long, graceful skirts that replace the severe, square lines they have been wearing since the beginning of the war.

With good reason, Dior calls his collection the 'New Look'.

HINDUS AND MOSLEMS AT WAR

April 1, Delhi While the British ruled India, the rivalry between Indian Hindus and Moslems was kept in check. With independence approaching, the struggle for power between the two sides has led to violent clashes all over this vast country. The death toll is rising daily and the police and the army are unable to keep order.

THE MARSHALL PLAN

June 5, Harvard, USA Speaking at Harvard University, the US Secretary of State, George Marshall, has outlined a plan to help Europe repair the damage of war. Billions of dollars will be made available to countries willing to co-operate with each other in order to bring about the economic recovery of Europe.

INDIANS AGREE TO BE DIVIDED

June 15, Delhi The leaders of the Hindu Congress Party and of the Moslem League have agreed to the Mountbatten plan for the partition of India.

Lord Mountbatten proposes that the country should be divided into two states: a new state to be called Pakistan for the Moslems, and the rest of India for the Hindus and Sikhs. British officials are beginning the complicated task of working out the details of how India will be divided into two nations. They have very little time. Lord Mountbatten has decided to bring forward Independence Day to August 15, in two months' time.

JEWS DEMAND PART OF PALESTINE

July 18, Jerusalem The agitation for an independent Jewish state to be set up in Palestine is growing. The British ruling authorities are caught between the Jews on the one hand and Arabs on the other. Both the Jews and Arabs claim the right to live in Palestine. Jews worldwide were outraged when the British authorities turned away a ship crowded with 5000 Jewish refugees from Europe, and refused to let them land.

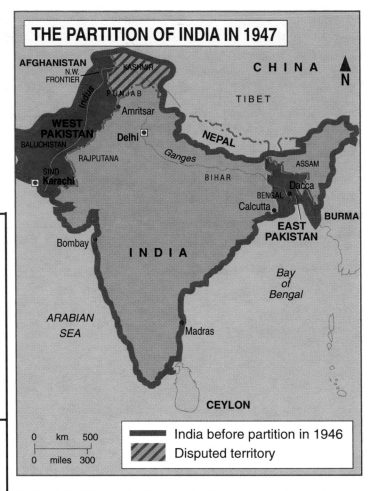

THE PARTITION OF INDIA IN 1947

- ——— India before partition in 1946
- /// Disputed territory

0 km 500
0 miles 300

NEW STATES BORN

Aug 15, Delhi and Karachi At midnight last night, British rule in India ended after 89 years, and two independent states, India and Pakistan, were born. Pandit Nehru becomes the prime minister of India, whose population is largely Hindu. Moslem Pakistan is to be led by Liaquat Ali Khan.

The independence celebrations have been marred by clashes between Hindus and Moslems.

Pandit Nehru (left) and Mahatma Gandhi.

THE TRUMAN DOCTRINE IN ACTION

Aug 31, Paris Sixteen European nations have met to prepare a response to the United States' offer of Marshall Aid. They are asking for $28 billion over four years. Much of the aid will be in the form of machinery and goods.

Neither Soviet Russia nor any of the Iron Curtain countries attended the meeting. They will not receive American aid. The US does not intend to help the Soviets recover. The Marshall Plan is part of the Truman Doctrine. In March, US President Harry S. Truman made a speech broadcast to the nation. In it, he challenged the power of the Communist countries. He undertook to support any nation against what he calls the tyranny of Communism. This policy makes plain the world is now divided into two hostile camps. The United States of America and her allies face the Communist countries led by Soviet Russia.

A German poster, which reads, 'An open road for The Marshall Plan', welcomes American financial help.

ROYAL WEDDING CHEERS GLOOMY LONDON

Nov 20, London Princess Elizabeth, heir to the British throne, was married today to Lieutenant Philip Mountbatten. The wedding took place in Westminster Abbey. It was televised and broadcast to millions of people all over the world.

The bride and bridegroom are distant cousins. Both are descended from Queen Victoria. Lt. Mountbatten's uncle is Lord Louis Mountbatten, now Governor General of the new state of India.

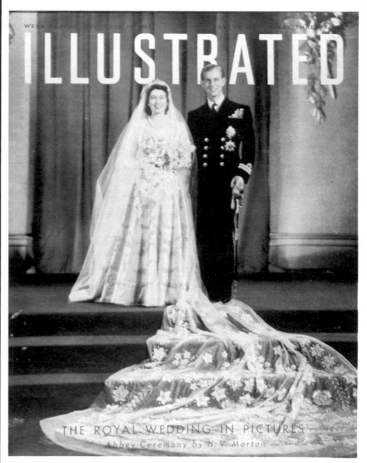

Cover story: the royal wedding

SEPARATE STATES IN PALESTINE

Dec 31, Jerusalem Last month the United Nations General Assembly approved a plan to create both an Arab and a Jewish state in Palestine. The Jews are in favour. The Arab states and the Arabs of Palestine oppose it.

The new states will come into being when the forces of the ruling British leave in May next year.

HUGE COMPUTER IN OPERATION

Dec 30, Pennsylvania, USA The world's first all-electronic digital computer has been installed at the University of Pennsylvania. It has 18,000 valves, several kilometres of copper wire, fills a large room and weighs thirty tons. The computer performs complicated calculations at a dizzying speed. Already, however, work is going on to produce machines which are more compact.

INDEPENDENCE DEATH TOLL

Dec 31, Indo-Pakistani border The final group of Moslem refugees from India has crossed into Pakistan. The division of India created over eight million refugees, as Hindus living in Pakistan and Moslems trapped in India fled in terror to their new national homelands. Over 400,000 people may have lost their lives in the turmoil that followed independence.

NEWS IN BRIEF . . .

HENRY FORD DIES

April 17, Detroit, USA Henry Ford, pioneer of the motor car, the man who put America on wheels, has died aged 82. Henry Ford co-founded the Ford Motor Company in 1903, and by 1908 was mass-producing the famous Model T. His new assembly-line methods enabled the car to be sold at $500, making it within the reach of many American families.

Mr. Henry Ford beside his Model T.

THE KON TIKI ADVENTURE

Nov 30, Tahiti, Pacific Norwegian scientist Thor Heyerdahl, with five companions, has recently landed on an island near here after drifting for 8000 km (5000 miles) across the Pacific. The voyage began in Peru 3½ months ago and was made on the *Kon Tiki*, a raft built of balsawood logs. Mr. Heyerdahl claims that the journey supports his theory that the peoples of the Pacific came from South America, rather than from Asia as is generally supposed.

The *Kon Tiki* in the Pacific.

FRANCO'S PLANS FOR SPAIN

July, Madrid Since the civil war ended in 1939, General Franco has ruled Spain. But his brand of Fascism is not popular. The United Nations has so far excluded Spain, so Franco is planning reforms. He issued a declaration of human rights in 1945 and this month asked every citizen whether they wanted a monarch on the throne. Most Spaniards said they did. Despite these moves away from Facism towards a freer regime, Spain will receive nothing from America under the Marshall Plan to repair war damage.

1948

Jan 30   **Assassination of Mahatma Gandhi**
May 14   **State of Israel born**
June 24   **Russia blockades West Berlin**
July 5   **National Health Service launched in Britain**
Nov 3   **President Truman re-elected**

EAST AND WEST AT ODDS OVER GERMANY

Jan 18, Berlin   The wartime allies, the Americans, the British and the French, have occupied the western part of Germany since the war ended. Now they have introduced a new currency in the parts of Germany they occupy.

The Russians have objected strongly. They claim that the western powers are trying to make western Germany into a new state which will be on their side, and hostile to Soviet Russia.

PEACEMAKER ASSASSINATED

Jan 30, New Delhi   Mahatma Gandhi, the man who used peaceful means to make India free, is dead. He was shot today while on his way to pray for peace between Hindus and Moslems in India. His killer, a young Hindu, was seized on the spot.

INDIA MOURNS GANDHI

Jan 31, New Delhi   According to Hindu custom, Mahatma Gandhi's body was cremated today. His funeral pyre was lit beside the waters of the sacred River Jumna. It was decked with beautiful flowers. Over a million mourners joined the eight-kilometre (five-mile) funeral procession. The ashes were cast into the waters where the Rivers Jumna and Ganges meet.

Police who have questioned Mr. Gandhi's killer say he belongs to a group of Hindus who violently oppose the Mahatma's message of peace and goodwill between Moslems and Hindus in India.

Trouble has broken out in a number of Indian cities following the Mahatma's death. Police were forced to open fire on rioters in parts of Bombay.

The ashes from Gandhi's funeral pyre were taken on a coach decorated like a temple. The urn went through a crowd of over a million mourners.

RUSSIANS CUT OFF WEST BERLIN

June 24, Berlin Berlin lies in the eastern half of Germany which is controlled by the Russians. Today, the Russians have closed all the roads, railways and canals that link Berlin with the west. They hope that by cutting off supplies, they will force the western powers to give up the parts of the city they occupy. If the Russians succeed, the whole of Berlin will be under Soviet control.

HUGE AIRLIFT TO BERLIN

June 30, Berlin The former allies are running a huge airlift to bring essential supplies into Berlin. They want to prevent Berlin falling wholly into Russian hands. Cargo planes are landing every four minutes in the city, carrying food, fuel and medical supplies.

The western powers have no intention of giving up Berlin. "We are in Berlin to stay," says America's Secretary of State, George Marshall.

PALESTINE IN TURMOIL

May 15, Jerusalem Yesterday, at 4 p.m., eight hours before the last Briton was due to leave Palestine, the Jews announced that the new state of Israel had been born. Israel will have to fight for its life. Troops from five Arab nations, Egypt, Transjordan, Iraq, Syria and Lebanon, are preparing to invade the new state. The United Nations is now responsible for keeping the peace in Palestine.

NO END TO THE WAR IN PALESTINE

Oct 15, Jerusalem Fighting has been going on for most of the summer between Israelis and Arabs from surrounding countries. Twice the UN has arranged a ceasefire, and twice the two sides have used the truce as an opportunity to build up fresh stocks of weapons and ammunition. The conflict has begun again as Israeli troops attack Egyptian forces in the desert around the port of Gaza.

TRUMAN TRIUMPHS

Nov 3, Washington   Harry S. Truman has been elected president of the United States. Every opinion poll forecast a victory for his opponent, but Truman has proved them all wrong.

Mr. Truman is already the president. The office passed to him, as vice-president, nearly four years ago. He moved to the White House as president when Franklin D. Roosevelt died in 1945.

BERLIN WILL NOT BE STARVED OUT

Dec 31, Berlin   The Soviet blockade of Berlin continues, and so does the western airlift into the city. The quantity of supplies reaching Berlin is increasing as the airlift becomes more efficient, and as larger aircraft are used in the operation. Unless the Russians are prepared to risk war by shooting down the transport aircraft, the western powers will remain in Berlin.

THE LONDON OLYMPICS

August 16, London   After a gap of 12 years, caused by the war, the Olympic Games have returned. The 1948 games, held in London, have just ended.

The organizers were too short of money, and time, to build an Olympic village to house the athletes, or to construct new stadiums in which the events might take place. Nevertheless, some outstanding performances were produced in these shabby surroundings. Mrs. Fanny Blankers-Koen from Holland won four track events. The most impressive race was run by the Czech soldier Emil Zatopek, who set a new Olympic record on the track in the 10,000 metres. He came in nearly a lap ahead of the next runner.

FIGHTING AT GAZA

December 31, Jerusalem   The Israelis are successfully defending their new land against the Arabs. They have almost cleared the north of the country of Arab troops and have knocked Lebanon, Syria, Iraq and Transjordan out of the conflict. Fighting is now concentrated in the south of the country. The Israelis have entered Egyptian territory and have cut off an Egyptian army near Gaza. All attempts by the UN to persuade the two sides to call off the fighting have failed.

The 'Flying Dutchwoman', Mrs. Fanny Blankers-Koen (on the right) on the way to winning one of four gold medals at the London Olympics.

NEWS IN BRIEF . . .

PRINCESS ELIZABETH HAS A SON

Nov 14, London Princess Elizabeth, heir to the British throne, has given birth to her first child, a son. The baby prince is to be named Charles and is next in line to the throne after his mother.

BURMA GAINS ITS INDEPENDENCE FROM BRITAIN

Jan 4, Rangoon Today at exactly 4.20 a.m. local time, Burma became independent. Burmese astrologers chose the time and date in order to bring the new country good luck. The ceremony ended British control dating back to 1886.

The Japanese occupied Burma in the recent war until British and Indian forces drove them out. The British returned but the Burmese were opposed to all foreign rule.

TRANSISTORS REPLACE VALVES

Sept, New York A revolution in electronics is about to begin. The Bell Telephone Laboratories in USA have invented the 'transistor'. This tiny part will replace valves in radios. It is much smaller, can be re-used, and does not overheat. One day, radios may be produced which are small enough to carry around.

Researchers into the new science of computing also see transistors as a major breakthrough in making computers smaller, more reliable, more robust and economical.

A NATIONAL HEALTH SERVICE IN BRITAIN

July 5, London From today, everyone in Britain qualifies for free medical and dental treatment. False teeth, medicines and pills, even wigs, will be supplied free under the new system. Doctors and dentists have fought hard to stop the scheme from being set up. They claim that patients will receive worse care than they have now.

Britain's Labour Government has gone ahead, in spite of these objections. The man who has done most to bring free health care to all is the Minister for Health, Mr. Aneurin Bevan.

Poor health among Britain's slums should be relieved by the new National Health Service.

1949

Feb 24   Egypt and Israel sign armistice
April 4   NATO treaty signed
May 12   Russia lifts Berlin blockade
May 26   China's Communists take Shanghai
May 27   Apartheid policy adopted in South Africa
Oct 1   Mao leads People's Republic of China

COMMUNISTS CAPTURE PEKING

Jan 21, Peking China's long civil war seems almost over. The conflict between the Nationalists and Communists began more than 20 years ago. The Japanese invasion interrupted it, but since the Japanese left China after losing in World War II, the two sides have returned to the struggle.

Today, the Communist army led by Mao Tse-tung entered the capital, Peking. Chiang Kai-shek's Nationalists have been routed. General Chiang himself has retired, leaving the command of the Nationalist forces to younger men unknown to the outside world.

Mao's forces are now advancing to attack the last great Nationalist stronghold, the city of Shanghai.

ARMISTICE IN THE MIDDLE EAST

Feb 24, Rhodes, Greece The Egyptians and Israelis have at last signed a peace treaty. The fighting in the Middle East is ended – for the time being.

The Israelis have won a great victory. Three-quarters of what used to be Palestine is now part of the state of Israel. Not enough remains to form a state for the Arabs who live there. Over 700,000 Arabs fled during the fighting. They live in harsh, poor conditions in the Arab countries around Israel's borders. About 160,000 stayed in their homes and are now under Israeli rule.

Conflict between Arabs and Jews is even greater than before the war. Peace in the Middle East is as far off as ever. The war solved nothing.

Palestinian refugees leave their homes to seek temporary shelter.

A TREATY TO DEFEND WESTERN NATIONS

April 4, Washington, USA Eleven countries from North America and Western Europe have signed a treaty to form a new peace alliance. It is to be known as the North Atlantic Treaty Organization, or NATO for short. If one country is attacked, the others will come to its aid. NATO members include the United States, Canada, Britain, France, Italy, Holland and Denmark.

The obvious purpose of the treaty is to make an attack by the Soviet Union or its allies less likely.

'WHITES FIRST' PARTY WINS IN SOUTH AFRICA

May 27, Pretoria The Nationalist Party won yesterday's election on the slogan 'Apartheid'. It means 'separation'. South African laws already favour white people. Most non-whites do not have a vote, they may not travel freely nor live where they like. Under apartheid, they will become a separate race of second-class citizens. New laws promised by the Nationalists will make non-whites little more than slaves in their own country, one of the richest in the world.

MAO TSE-TUNG, MASTER OF CHINA

May 26, Shanghai Today, white victory flags are flying all over Shanghai as the Communists march in. The long battle for China is over.

Some clearing-up remains to be done, but there is no doubt now that Mao Tse-tung and the Communists are masters of China.

BERLIN BLOCKADE LIFTED

May 12, New York Russia has agreed to lift the Berlin blockade. A settlement was reached at the United Nations after lengthy talks between the USSR and the western former allies.

This is a great victory for the West. Not only has the blockade been beaten, but the Soviet Union has agreed to the creation of West Germany as a separate state. It will be formed from the zones of Germany occupied by the Americans, the French and the British.

There is delight and relief in Berlin at this news. Lorry-loads of food and other supplies are already on their way through Soviet-controlled territory.

NATIONALISTS FLEE MAINLAND CHINA

July 16, Formosa The last Nationalist forces have left China and have fled to the island of Formosa, 100 km off the Chinese coast. Here the Nationalist leader General Chiang Kai-shek is setting up a new independent republic. The General has given the island its ancient Chinese name, 'Taiwan'.

CHINA JOINS COMMUNIST CAMP

Oct 1, Peking, China Soviet Russia has gained a mighty ally. Today, Mao Tse-tung has proclaimed China a Communist Republic. He himself is to be head of the new state with the title of Chairman of the People's Republic. His friend and colleague Chou En-lai is to be Premier and Foreign Minister.

The United States supported the Nationalists in China's civil war. The Communist victory is therefore an American defeat. China's 540 million people are a huge addition to the strength of Communism in Asia and throughout the world.

STEEP FALL IN VALUE OF STERLING

Sept 18, London Yesterday a British pound would buy 4.03 dollars. Today, it is only worth $2.80. This announcement of a 30.5 per cent drop in the value of the pound has shocked financial markets all over the world.

NEWS IN BRIEF . . .

BETTER SOUND – BUT AT A PRICE!

Jan 15, New York Music lovers in the United States can now listen to their favourite works on seven-inch (180 mm) 'unbreakable' gramophone records. Unfortunately, there are two kinds of record, and they are made to revolve at different speeds. Existing 12-inch (300 mm) records go round at a higher speed than either of them.

If music lovers want to play the new records, they will have to buy expensive new equipment on which to play them.

NO MORE COUPONS FOR CLOTHES

Feb 1, London Better times are coming to Britain. Clothes rationing has ended after eight years. Price controls will stay, however. The Government has promised to freeze prices if shops try to increase them.

NKRUMAH HEADS NEW AFRICAN PARTY

Oct, Gold Coast A new political party has been launched in the Gold Coast (Ghana). The Convention People's Party, led by Kwame Nkrumah, aims to organize African people at village level. When they are politically ready, they will fight for independence from European colonials. They will use strikes and boycotts – every means other than armed rebellion. Mr. Nkrumah is a son of poor parents, but studied in America. After the liberation of his own country from Britain, he aims to bring all Africans into a peaceful union.

Race rioters in Durban, South Africa.

NINETEEN EIGHTY-FOUR

June 10, London In his latest book, *Nineteen Eighty-Four*, George Orwell makes nightmare predictions about the state of the world in the year of the book's title, 1984. There are three superstates in that world and they are endlessly at war with each other. There is no freedom. All activities are controlled; even thoughts are monitored, by the Thought Police. Those who displease the State are taken away to an unknown fate.

It seems Mr. Orwell had Stalin's Russia in mind when he wrote *Nineteen Eighty-Four*.

SWEDISH NEUTRALITY SHUNNED

Nov, Stockholm Sweden has recently proposed a defence pact with the other Scandinavian countries, Norway and Denmark. But the proposal has been rejected; Norway and Denmark are to join NATO. Sweden will remain neutral. At the end of the war, Sweden was a rich country; Norway and Denmark were both devastated by the war.

RACE RIOTS IN DURBAN

Jan 15, Durban, South Africa Over 200 troops and armed police are on guard in Durban. Riots started when it was claimed an Indian shopkeeper attacked a small black boy. Black Africans then took revenge on the Indian population, particularly shopkeepers. Produce rotted in Durban market as Indian shopkeepers were too scared to buy it. About 105 non-whites have died in the fighting.

CANADA'S NEW PROVINCE

Oct, Montreal Canada has a new province. The former British colony Newfoundland has opted to join Canada which is a thriving young country.

Although Canadians took an active part in the last war, their industry at home thrived. Canada supplied arms and food to the Allies. Steel and aluminium plants worked full tilt, and are still booming. Timber, fishing and hydroelectric power are also very prosperous industries.

PEOPLE OF THE FORTIES

Dwight David Eisenhower 1890-1969

Eisenhower, or 'Ike' as he became known, was appointed to lead the Allied invasion of north Africa in 1942. He was well-liked by all ranks in the forces, and had a genius for making 'difficult' people work well together. In 1944 Ike commanded the Allied forces that landed in Europe, and continued in command until the war ended in 1945.

After the war, in 1952 and again in 1956, he was elected President of the United States of America. He continued Truman's policy of resisting the spread of Soviet Communism.

George Orwell, British author 1903–1950

George Orwell's real name was Eric Blair. He was born in India, went to school at Eton and became a writer. None of his books gained him either fame or fortune until, in 1945, he published *Animal Farm*. All his life, Orwell attacked injustice and oppression, whether it came from wealth or politics. On the surface, *Animal Farm* is a simple tale about a farmyard. It is also a savage attack on the evils of extreme left-wing socialism. *Nineteen Eighty-Four* followed: a novel about the hideous conditions in a world run by oppressive tyrants.

Harry S. Truman 1884–1972

Harry S. Truman was a farmer's son from Missouri, USA. He fought in World War I and later went into politics. In 1944 Roosevelt chose him as vice-president. A year later, Truman became president when Roosevelt died. Truman faced huge and difficult decisions. He authorized the use of the atomic bomb to end the war against Japan. He led America to head the alliance of the powers against Soviet Communism. In 1948, Truman was elected president for a second term. In America, the presidents who followed him frequently sought his advice.

Winston Churchill 1874–1965

Winston Churchill was born to a British aristocratic family. His father was English, his mother was American. He became a soldier and fought in colonial wars in India and Africa. He went to the Boer War as a newspaper reporter. In 1900, he entered Parliament and was a member of the Government during World War I. Churchill became unpopular after the war. Many thought him a dangerous warmonger because of his constant warnings of the threat posed by Soviet Communism and, later, by Nazi Germany. In 1940, aged 66, Churchill became Prime Minister and led the British to victory in 1945. He was voted out of power in 1945 and turned to writing. He won the Nobel Prize for Literature in 1953. He became Prime Minister again in 1951, but resigned because of ill-health in 1955.

Charles De Gaulle 1890–1970

A hero of World War I, de Gaulle fled to England when the Germans conquered France in 1940. From London he organized the Free French in resistance to the Germans. In 1944 he led French forces in triumph through the streets of Paris when the Allies liberated the city. He held France together in the troubled times after the war and later became President of his country.

Viscount Montgomery, soldier 1887–1970

Montgomery became famous as 'Monty', the British leader of the 8th Army in Egypt. Born Bernard Law, and the son of a bishop, Montgomery trained at Sandhurst. He fought in World War I, and was wounded. At the start of World War II he commanded the 3rd Division in France until they were evacuated from Dunkirk. It was in 1942 that he was given command of the 8th Army in Egypt. He swiftly re-equipped the forces and restored their morale. He launched the Battle of El Alamein in October, against Rommel's forces. The week-long battle ended in the first great Allied victory, and was a turning point in the progress of the war.

For the first time ever

1940	USA	Automatic gearbox developed
		First Jeep produced
		Penicillin produced in quantity
	UK	Plutonium discovered
		Inflatable life jacket for airmen developed (called the Mae West)
1941	USA	Portable two-way radio in use
		Television advertisements first seen
	UK	Terylene produced
1942	USA	Napalm tested
	Germany	Long range rockets developed
1943	France	Aqualung developed
	UK	Programmable electronic computer in use
	USA	Streptomycin discovered
		Teflon developed
1944	Germany	Air to air missiles developed
		Ground to air missiles also used
		Nerve gases developed
1945	Holland	Artificial kidneys available for patients
	USA	Atomic bomb first exploded
		Microwave oven in use
		Tupperware boxes invented
		Zoom lens used in photography
	UK	Contact lenses developed
1946	UK	Artificial ski ramp used
	France	Bikini swimsuit revealed
	USA	Electric windows (for cars) available
	Italy	Espresso coffee machine in use
1947	UK	Land Rover designed
	USA	Polaroid camera developed
		First piloted supersonic flight
		Tubeless tyres on sale

1948	USA	McDonalds hamburgers on sale
		Long-playing record developed
		'Scrabble', the word board game, on the market
	UK	Soluble aspirin available
		Heated rear windows (for cars) available
	Switzerland	'Velcro' fastening tape developed
1949	USA	High altitude rocket tested
		Key starting (for cars) available
	UK	First jet powered airliner – the Comet – flies

New words and expressions

Wartime activities introduced many new words into the English language. Most fell out of use when the war ended. Some of those that remain are included in this list of 1940s words:

air sea rescue
airstrip
apartheid
backroom boy or girl
bale out (from an aircraft)
bebop
bomb-blast
blip
blitz
bug (to plant a listening device)
cannibalize
D-Day
earth-shaking
fast-talking
flight-control
flying saucer
freebie

Geiger counter
gremlin
hassle
junkie
loo
microfiche
napalm
pin-up
potty chair
radar
remote-control
scorched earth policy
squat (an illegally occupied house or flat)
Technicolor
up-date
walkie-talkie
wolf-whistle

How many of these words and expressions do we still use today? Do you know what they all mean?

Glossary

armistice: an agreement between opposing sides to stop fighting.

armour: toughening to the sides of tanks or other vehicles to protect them.

Axis: the Axis powers in World War II were Germany and its allies.

Balkans: a group of countries in south-east Europe: Bulgaria, Hungary, Greece, Romania, Albania and Yugoslavia.

barrage: a large number of guns shelling the same target together.

battleship: a large warship, usually over 30,000 tonnes, protected by thick armour and armed with a number of heavy guns.

blitzkrieg: a violent attack by land and air forces intended to win a quick victory. A German word meaning 'lightning war'. The shortened form 'blitz' means the night attacks on British cities by the German airforce.

carrier: short for aircraft carrier.

convoy: a number of merchant ships travelling together, under the protection of warships.

curfew: a regulation requiring people to stay indoors at particular times, usually at night.

Free-French: a group of French politicians and soldiers who escaped from France when Germany conquered it in 1940.

Luftwaffe: the German airforce; in German Luftwaffe means 'air weapon'.

marines: troops trained to fight on land or sea.

partition: to partition a country is to divide it into parts, with separate governments.

'Red': another word for 'communist'. Soviet Russia was a communist country and its army was often called the 'Red Army'.

Russian Revolution: the revolution of 1917 which made the Communists the rulers of Russia.

Singapore: a large port on an island at the southern tip of the Malay peninsula. In the forties, Singapore was part of the British Commonwealth. It was a huge naval base which was vital to the defence of British territory and trade in south-east Asia.

Tobruk: a port in Libya on the Mediterranean. Tobruk changed hands four times during the war in north Africa. Both the Axis and the Allied armies used it as a supply base.

Ukraine: part of the former Soviet Union; now an independent state. It is rich in coal and minerals, and the largest wheat-growing area in Europe. Hitler invaded the Soviet Union largely to gain control of the wealth of the Ukraine.

United Nations: an international organization set up during the war by the Allies to keep peace in the world once the war was over.

White House: the official residence, in Washington, of the President of the United States of America.

Zionist: in the forties, a Zionist was a Jew who supported the setting up of an independent state for Jews in Palestine.

Further Reading

The Twentieth Century World: Peter and Mary Speed. Oxford University Press 1982

Britain at War: Ian Gilmour. Oliver and Boyd 1989

Echoes of the Second World War: Trish Marx. Macdonald Childrens' Books 1989

Hitler and the Third Reich: Catherine Bradley. Watts 1990

Russia under Stalin: Michael Gibson. Wayland 1972

Great Lives of the Twentieth Century: ed Alan Bullock. Weidenfeld 1981

Hiroshima: Marion Yass. Wayland 1984

Growing up in the Post-War 40s: N. L. Fyson. Batsford 1988

Picture History of the 20th Century; the 1940s: Tim Wood and R. J. Unstead. Watts 1990

Index

Afrika Corps 13, 16, 19
apartheid 40
atom bomb 26, 29

Baden Powell, Robert 14
Baird, John L. 30
Battle of Britain 10
Belsen 25
Berlin 24, 27, 35, 36, 37, 40
Bevan, Aneurin 38
Bismarck 12
blitz 11, 14
Burma 26, 38

Canada 41
Chamberlain, Neville 8
Chaplin, Charles 11
Chiang Kai-shek 27, 39, 40
China 27, 29, 39, 40
Churchill, Winston 8, 10, 14, 19,
    25, 27, 43
Cold War 31
Cologne 17

D Day 21
De Gaulle, Charles 10, 23, 43
Denmark 8
Disney, Walt 14
Dunkirk 9

Eisenhower, Dwight D. 21, 24, 42
El Alamein 14, 16
Elizabeth, Princess 33, 38

Ford, Henry 34
France 8, 9, 10, 17, 21, 22, 29, 43
Franco, Francisco 34

Gandhi, Mahatma 29, 35
Goering, Hermann 28
Germany 8, 9, 10, 11, 12, 14, 15,
    16, 17, 18, 19, 21, 22, 23, 24, 25,
    27, 28, 29, 35, 36, 37, 43

Hindus 30, 32, 34, 35
Hiroshima 26
Hitler, Adolf 10, 11, 12, 23, 24
Holland (Netherlands) 8
Hong Kong 23

Iron Curtain 29
Israel 35, 36, 37, 39
Italy 13, 18, 19, 22

Japan 13, 16, 23, 24, 26
Johnson, Amy 14

Kon Tiki 34
Kursk 18

Labour Party 27
Lascaux 9
Leyte Gulf 23
Luftwaffe 8, 10, 15

Mao Tse-tung 39, 40
Marshall Plan 32, 33

Mexico 10, 20
Moscow 12
Montgomery, Bernard 16, 43
Moslems 30, 32, 34, 35
Mountbatten, Lord Louis 31, 32
Mountbatten, Philip 33
Mussolini, Benito 24

Nagasaki 26
National Health Service 38
Nazis 8, 28, 29
Nehru, Pandit 32
New Look 31
Nkrumah, Kwame 41
Norway 8

Olympic Games 37
Orwell, George 41, 42

Palestine 28, 32, 33, 36, 37, 39
Paris 10, 21, 22, 30, 31, 33, 43
Pearl Harbor 13
Peking 39, 40
Philippines 13, 16, 23
Poland 8, 19, 21, 22
prefabs 23

Quisling, Vidkung 8

rationing 17, 30, 41
Red Army (Russian) 12, 15, 18, 22,
    23, 24
refugees 32, 39
Rommel, Erwin 13, 16
Roosevelt, Franklin D. 10, 14, 19,
    27
Royal Air Force 10, 17, 21
Royal Navy 8, 9, 12, 13
Russia (USSR) 8, 9, 15, 18, 19, 20,
    21, 22, 27, 28, 31, 33, 35, 36, 37,
    40

Singapore 16
Slim, William 26
South Africa 37, 40
Spaak, Paul Henri 28
Stalin, Joseph 10, 19
Stalingrad 15

Taiwan 40
Tobruk 13
Trotsky, Lev 10
Truman, Harry S. 27, 33, 37
United Kingdom 8, 9, 10, 11, 12,
    14, 17, 20, 23, 25, 27, 30, 31, 33,
    37, 38, 40, 41
United Nations Organization 27,
    29, 33, 36, 37
United States of America 10, 13,
    14, 17, 18, 22, 23, 24, 25, 27, 28,
    37, 39, 40

VE Day 25
Vietnam 29

Warsaw 19, 22